STILL BY YOUR SIDE

*How I Know a Great Love
Never Dies*

MARJORIE HOLMES

A Crossroad Book
The Crossroad Publishing Company
New York

Grateful acknowledgment to Chosen Books, Inc., a division of
Baker Book House Company, Grand Rapids, Michigan,
for permission to use an excerpt from *To Live Again*
by Catherine Marshall.

1996

The Crossroad Publishing Company
370 Lexington Avenue, New York, NY 10017

Printed in the United States of America

Library of Congress Cataloging-in-Publication Data

Holmes, Marjorie, 1910-
    Still by your side : how I know a great love never dies / Marjorie
Holmes.
        p.   cm.
    ISBN 0-8245-1631-1 (hc)
    1. Consolation. 2. Bereavement — Religious aspects — Christianity.
3. Holmes, Marjorie, 1910-   . 4. Christian biography — United
States.   I. Title.
BV4905.2.H588   1996
248.8'6'092–dc20
    [B]   96-31324
                                                              CIP

STILL BY
YOUR SIDE

CONTENTS

Chapter One

THE MUSIC BOX

PRAYER OF BLESSING

Dear Lord,

Please bless everyone who reads this book.

Especially those who have lost someone

they deeply loved.

Let it help to comfort them.

Let it reassure them

that if both their love and their faith are strong,

they *will* be together again in Paradise!

*I*T BEGAN with the music box. The faint sweet tinkling sounds that woke me one night after my husband's death.

It was the first time I had been alone since the funeral; the big Tudor house was finally quiet, utterly quiet after the commotion of voices these past few weeks. The sounds of people coming and going, trying to comfort me with gifts of food and flowers and offers of help. Friends, neighbors, the clergy, members of George's family, who didn't live far; and my own scattered four who'd stayed with me as long as possible before driving or flying back to their homes. I had just put the last one on the plane: my oldest daughter, Mickie, who pleaded, "Mother, are you *sure* you'll be all right?"

"Of course, honey. Don't worry. I'll be fine!"

Exhausted and a little scared, but actually relieved, I unlocked the silent, empty house, took a hot bath, and plunged into bed, determined to sleep. But I was just drifting off, it seemed, when I heard that delicate music tinkling. Puzzled, I roused, and lifted my head to listen, heart pounding. "Don't be silly," I warned myself. "Don't start *hearing* things! You've been through so much, you're dreaming, go back to *sleep*."

I pulled the covers over my ears and tried, but the dainty tinkling persisted, like tiny angels playing harps. Half-protesting, I knew I'd have to find its source. Had somebody left the radio on? No, I'd have heard it when I came in. Besides, our only radio was downstairs, and this was close.

Close. My heart beat faster. The music box!

No, no, impossible, ridiculous. It hasn't played in years; you'll only be disappointed. But out of curiosity and the need to be sure, I got up and ran to the dresser where I kept the small white gilded box I had bought George for our first Valentine's Day, the year we were married. Its sparkling, haunting little love song became a part of our bedtime ritual, after reading aloud and praying, or even making love. The last thing we heard before we fell asleep.

But gradually its sweet melody weakened, and finally, after a few years, it stopped altogether. And when I took it back to the store, I was told it couldn't be fixed, or even replaced. "The Valentine models don't last very long," the salesman said.

The company didn't even make them any more. I couldn't bear to part with it, however. It was such a pretty little thing, all gold and white and silver, with a beautiful poem inside, which George would also read and sing to me.

But now *something* was playing somewhere, almost as if that plaintive little tune was *calling* me! Scarcely daring to hope, I scurried across the carpeting and opened the lid.

"George, George!" I screamed, and began to cry. For that little box was playing for me as clearly and sweetly as it had played for us the very first time we heard it together almost eleven years before.

And even now, several years after his death, it still sometimes plays for me.

I sometimes hear that delicate tinkling in the night, usually when I'm worried about a problem or preparing for something important the following day. I never open the box otherwise. I don't feel its music is mine to seek, only to receive. A thrilling reassurance that the wonderful man who sang to me from the moment we met, to almost his last hour on earth, is sending our little lost song to help and encourage me now. To tell me that he still loves me and someday will sing to me again!

And one morning, to my astonishment, I heard the box tinkling away right after I'd received good news. And when I ran to open the lid, that dear little thing was playing with such joy and fervor I burst into tears. For I knew with all my heart that George was celebrating with me.

This miracle of the music box was the first of a number of remarkable things that have happened to me since losing the greatest love of my life — experiences for which there is no logical explanation, but rather evidence, at least for me, that a truly great love on earth will not perish even in death. If the bond of love has been very strong, it can't be broken; there will still be communion between the two who parted, and when God is ready, their souls will be together forever in Paradise.

To me this is so significant that I want to share these experiences as I describe my life without George and what I have learned from grief. Actually, such things are not uncommon, and they can be beautiful, if received as a gift from the God who created us and Jesus who promised us eternal life. *But they must not be sought or contrived.* I can't warn you too strongly: beware of anyone who would claim to induce them, hear them for you, or interpret their meaning. Such people are not God's messengers. At best they are fallible human beings, who may mean well, but are woefully misguided; at worst, false prophets, as condemned in the Bible, who could lead you astray.

I know, because once long ago, when I was young and vulnerable, I briefly followed that precarious path. But within a year I was seriously disillusioned, and learned a bitter lesson which I think God must have meant me to have, in order to warn others.

And now I want to introduce you to the husband for whom I was grieving that night of the music box. He had told me so many wonderful things during our marriage, and would tell me even more after he was gone.

Chapter Two

REMEMBERING
GEORGE

A Marriage Made in Heaven

Dear Lord,

How can I ever thank you

for this remarkable man?

The mystery and magic

of how he even *found* me;

and our marriage four months later!

It *was* a marriage made in heaven.

And although you've taken him home,

I know that when you are ready,

we will be together there in Paradise forever.

*H*IS EYES were blue — so blue. Never have I seen such blue eyes in a man. His hair, dark in his youth, was now gray, but still thick and curly. He had a small moustache. Earlier, people said, they used to call him Errol Flynn; later, another Tom Selleck. He had the most beautiful male voice I've ever heard. I teased him, "If you ever want to quit medicine, I'll be your manager. We'll go on the road, and look out, Kenny Rogers!"

He was over six feet tall, with a magnificent body. Once a champion athlete for Pitt. Captain of the swimming team, cross-country runner. His dresser was filled with gold medals. A beloved suburban Pittsburgh doctor, who'd been happily married for nearly fifty years. . . . The story of how we met is almost legendary, it's been told so often — in *People Magazine, Guideposts,* and my book *Second Wife, Second Life.* But I will repeat it briefly here.

Eight months after losing his wife, George was still mad with grief. Actually suicidal. He had tried it once before, stopped only by their big golden Lab, who barked wildly and leaped, knocking the sleeping pills from his hand. And this time, on that first

New Year's Eve alone, as he sorted her things in their bedroom, he was planning to proceed. But at midnight, just as the Old Year turned into 1981, something impelled him to fall to his knees and reach into his wife's closet, to the very bottom.

And there he found my book *I've Got to Talk to Somebody, God*. He read it all night and swore it saved his life.

Nonetheless, he was still despondent. And in February, at his children's insistence, he set off for Florida, as the two had done every year, to visit friends, stopping en route to see his son, an attorney in Silver Spring, Maryland, near Washington, D.C. There, George discovered that the author of this book lived somewhere in the Capitol area and had lost her husband the year before.

Although George had never even written to an author, he went to great lengths to find me, in spite of an unlisted number. My phone rang one day, and a rich male voice announced, "Marjorie Holmes? You saved my life. I love you!"

Shocked but intrigued, I listened, truly sorry I couldn't see him. "I'm just now leaving," I said, "on a two weeks' speaking trip."

"I'll wait!" he declared.

"Oh, no," I laughed, "you can't do that — go on to Florida."

"I'll wait," he repeated.

To my astonishment, he did. The day after I got home he arrived at my door, this tall handsome prince, with his arms full of roses. He asked me to marry him that first night. And although I told him, "No, George, you're still in love with your wife," after two dates and a week at Ocean City, Maryland, we were married — on the Fourth of July, four months from the day we met. He never did get to Florida that year.

It was a fairytale marriage. One tabloid which told our story featured him as "the most romantic man in the world." This much was true: fresh flowers on the table every morning. Love songs morning and evening. Love notes every day. And more....

George continued his medical practice; I continued to write. Yet in his zest for life he insisted that play is just as important as work. "Work and play, love and pray, in equal measure." Balance, he called it. "The secret of a happy life." We swam, we danced, we traveled: to some of their favorite places, like Bermuda and the other islands; or to my favorite, which was Europe. We ran the dogs across the Pittsburgh hills, climbed the cliffs at our summer home on Lake Erie, vigorous and carefree, joyful as children.

But there were serpents lurking in Paradise.

They spared us five magical years before they coiled; then every two years, as if on schedule, they began to strike my precious husband: blocked arteries to one leg, even though George had never smoked and did not have diabetes — two of the major causes of blockages.

And then gangrene. Desperate attempts to save the right leg; then the left. Surgery for lung cancer. Hospitals began to seem like home. Yet nothing diminished our delight in each other.... "In sickness and in health." Every day was to be treasured.

Finally, amputation of his left leg could be postponed no longer. Holding my hand and singing his usual love song, he was taken to surgery. And singing, however weakly, he returned, bravely waving his stump.

This was in September. Thanks to his indomitable spirit, he made a remarkable recovery. By spring he had adjusted to his prosthesis so well that he promised to dance with me at his fifty-fifth med school class reunion in Baltimore in May.

But even as we rejoiced, the serpents struck again. Return of his lung cancer. Breakdown of his other leg. Exactly a year from his first loss, the second leg was taken. We thought it might be easier this time, having gone through it before. We were wrong. But George was so courageous, his faith unshaken, his humor intact. He was still more fun sick than most people are well! — as I often told him. An inspiration to everyone who entered his room.

When he finally came home from the hospital, it was to a hospital bed and medical equipment in the living room. Here he resumed his precious ritual: love songs morning and evening; reading to me twice a day, and fervently writing his daily love notes. Though he could no longer pick or buy flowers for his breakfast bouquets, he would present me with a rose or a couple of tulips from the beautiful flowers others had sent us.

He was still very funny, sometimes wagging his

stumps like puppets and giving them voices, but profoundly aware of the tragedy of his loss. He was like a great bird grounded, wings spread but unable to fly. One day, gazing sadly down at those stumps, I heard him say, "Well, now the Lord has *really* brought me to my knees."

I slept on the couch beside him, where I could at least hold his hand. My own soul felt his growing despair, and he was very tired. One night at bedtime just before Christmas, as he was trying to sing "Goodnight, Sweetheart," his voice broke. He covered his face and groped for my hand. He couldn't finish.

The next day he went into a complete relapse and was rushed to the hospital. He died in January, semi-comatose after striving to write me one more love note.

⌣

Services were held in Canonsburg, Pennsylvania, the suburb where he had practiced so long. Still handsome, he was dressed all in blue, as his patients remembered him, his stethoscope and battered old doctor's bag beside him — and a copy of the book that had brought us together, *I've Got to Talk to Somebody, God.*

The night before our final goodbye, his family asked me to participate in a brief eulogy. I didn't think I could do it, but later I lay awake remembering how proudly he had always called me a pro. Pros don't cry in public. George had gone with me on so many promotion tours and speaking trips, I could do no less for him. And there were special things about my George that only I could tell them.

I said that I fell in love with him (as I know many women did) because he was so handsome and delightful. But not until I married him did I realize the brilliance of his mind: his wisdom, his imagination, his eloquence, his originality, his vivid descriptions and figures of speech. What a mate for a writer! Never before had I let anyone but editors read my manuscripts, but with George I could hardly wait. He had wonderful judgment, and he was a fountain of ideas. Some of the best ideas in my last four books, all written since our marriage, came from him.

"And he was so close to God," I recounted.

"Every morning he woke up at six o'clock and spent an hour just meditating and scribbling in what he called his *A–Z* books — an alphabetical journal of blessings." I held up one of the books and read a few of the blessings from the many listed under *L:* "Thank you, Lord, for *lungs,* that let us breathe 25,000 times a day.... *Light* bulbs, invented by Thomas A. Edison — how wonderful, turning night into day! *Lawyers,* what a help, especially my son Jeff. *Life,* the miracle of being on earth at all, a part of God's plan. *Laughter,* to brighten the journey and help heal our wonderful bodies. 'Better than a good medicine,' the Bible says. *Love,* God's greatest gift. Without love, life wouldn't be worth the struggle. But with love, how rewarding, what a joy! God is love, and with love we have God."

George and I had this joyful reward for ten years, six months, and twelve days. (He always counted them.) The eighth decade of both our lives. For me this final decade had been the happiest, most romantic, inspiring, and beautiful of all. But now the wedding feast was over. And the best wine *was* saved for the last.

Chapter Three

THE SECOND MIRACLE

THIS, MY GRIEF

This my grief, Lord — this, my grief!

I never knew what grief truly was before,

Because I had never truly loved before.

(Not like this, Lord — not like this!)

Though I had lost people dear to me before,

And missed them, yes — and grieved, I thought.

But not like this, Lord, not like this!

They did not take my heart with them.

(I have only one heart to give.)

They did not take my reason for living.

(I have only one life to live.)

They did not hold me in their arms at night

To love and comfort me to sleep.

Yes, of course I cried for them —

But this grief, Lord,

   Help me to bear it.

      I can't express it,

         I cannot speak,

            And it hurts too much,

               To *weep!*

THE SECOND MIRACLE began during the shock of those first days of being alone, utterly alone in this huge house where George had lived with his first wife for so long. This had troubled me when he first brought me here as a bride. I was shy and nervous, almost scared to change things, feeling like an intruder in another woman's home. But George had reassured me in a voice of real concern, "Marjorie, please remember — you *married a man who loves you*. You are lady of the house now. Do whatever you want." And with his help and encouragement, I got busy redecorating and refurbishing, and together we made it ours. This beautiful place where our lives would merge, one in body, soul, and *speech*.

Talking was almost as important to us as breathing, or even the joys of sex. We spoke the same language, almost read each other's thoughts. The house was never silent when George was there, and his radiant presence still filled it when he was away attending to his patients, or even later when he was so often a patient in the hospital himself. During those times I really didn't mind staying alone. I was too busy writing and telephoning or getting ready to go to see him, trying to remember what to take and all the things I wanted to tell him — because I had foolishly sold myself the sublime conviction that *he would be coming home.*

But the day of the final silence came. And with it the appalling realization: "I'll never see him again. I will never hear his voice, nor feel his arms around me!" It was impossible, paralyzing. I became a zombie, walking about performing my tasks, seeing but not seeing, hearing but not hearing, a puppet manipulated by unseen hands. Outwardly brisk, giving no sign, people said, but inwardly coping with an agony too monstrous to express.

How could this be happening to me? I am a stranger to grief, I realized astounded; I've never really known what sorrow *was* before! I had lost my parents, a brother I adored, and only twelve years ago my first husband, the father of my children. And yes, of course my heart was sad. I missed them. But never before had I suffered this helpless, hopeless, overwhelming anguish. For George was so special. There was nothing "of course" about him.

And never before had I been so close to another human being.

I would never have dreamed that the sudden joining of our lives would possess me so completely that I became a part of him. This time I had lost my soulmate; when he left he took my very soul with him. I felt stripped, literally vacated. My whole body and being, my womb, my loins, everything about me gone, leaving only this shell of a person who must behave, not sob or scream and pound the walls.

Except in secret when the pain is too great and nobody else can hear. And the suffering was compounded by this vacuum in which I drifted, numbed by the shock of realizing that for the first time in my life I would be *alone*.

I was raised in the noisy commotion of a family with four children, had roommates all through college, then married right after graduating and started a family of four children of my own, each one born five or six years apart, which prolonged the years of mothering. Our daughter Mickie was eighteen years old when her baby sister, Melanie, was born. And when my first husband died after forty-five years of marriage, Melanie and her husband were living in the house we had bought next door.

The following year I met and married George. During all those earlier years of raising a family while trying to write — constantly surrounded, forever on duty, forever interrupted — even one day by myself was a rare and precious treasure. Such bliss I even dreamed about at night, a vivid recurring dream in which I was living all by myself in a charming little white cottage perched on a mountaintop, where nobody else could find me unless I wanted, and I was free to write or read and do whatever I pleased as long as I pleased. A solitude so heavenly I hated to wake up.

But to be alone for even a day after living with George was not solitude but anguish. We had found each other so late and been so blindly happy. "And we haven't got that much *time,*" he had said from the beginning. The clocks of our lives were ticking, we had to make the most of every minute we could possibly have together.

Now I had to face the cruel fact that our time *had* run out. It was over! And this loneliness was so new to me I didn't know how. I would wander witless through the maze of the once lovely rooms which now seemed strange, empty, and lifeless without George. No longer beautiful — no longer even mine any more. I wasn't sure they ever had been. And again the anxious, half-apologetic sense of my own intrusion would rise up to haunt me. As if everything would always belong to the one who had been here first...and gone away first...and would be waiting for him. Her husband? My husband? Were they together now?

No, no, stop this! I knew I was stupid and silly, coping with questions it hurt too much to ask. None of my business. It also seemed ignoble somehow, almost unfair to the two who had worshiped each other all those years before I came along. If it hadn't been for *their* great love and marriage, I would never have been blessed with mine!

Besides, nobody on earth has the answers. Leave it up to God. Yet it didn't help to remember that the Bible says there will be no marriage or giving in marriage in heaven. I had trouble with that. I think a lot of people do. How could it be heaven without the beloved? I know my parents couldn't accept it, no matter how much they loved God. I will never forget how passionately they clutched each other the night my father died, sustained and comforted by their blind faith that they would never be parted again when her time came. My mother clung to that promise fiercely, even comically, the rest of her life. "If I can't be with Sam when I get there, I'm not staying!"

Despite these storms I counted my blessings as I worked at my desk, thanking God I could lose myself in my writing. And so grateful for George's son and daughter, who had always accepted me warmly and treated me beautifully. Now they called or dropped in almost every day, and they invited me for dinner as often as they could. But George II was a doctor like his dad, and daughter Diane chief microbiologist at the hospital. Both were very busy with their own families, as well as their professions. The last thing I wanted was for them to feel responsible for me. I cringed at the thought of ever becoming dependent on them or anyone.

So actually I did pretty well by day. But oh, how

I dreaded the long, lonely evenings, which began around five o'clock when it was time to feed the dogs and take them walking. I could hear our poodle's frenzied barking at the kitchen window, still expecting George to come driving in. They had always been eager to go, and Tanjy the poodle never stopped barking, even after George lost his legs. For this was the hour when I would fly into his arms, and we would take them with us, both Tanjy and Ben, the big golden Lab, who bounded together over the hills and meadows and along the stream, to circle the big schoolhouse below. While loving the earth and the sky and each other, George and I poured out everything that had happened to us all day.

Then "home to the hills," as George would sing as we started back, and to the dinner I'd already prepared fragrant in the oven, to be served by candlelight before an open fire he'd built in the gracious step-down living room. The soup and salad and his favorite dishes, which I tried to remember how to fix for him. Sometimes a fancy dessert I'd labored over as a special treat to surprise him.

I'd never cared much about cooking before, but

with George it was almost fun. Such meals were a kind of love-making between us: the eager gift of my efforts — and his appreciation, his thanks, his lavish compliments, the delight he seemed to take in every little thing.

Memories came flooding, cruel-sweet with nobody to cook for any more, nobody to feed but Tanjy and the big golden cat that appeared at our doorstep two days after we'd had to put Ben to sleep. Poor Tanjy. The dogs had been bosom buddies for thirteen years, born the same day and inseparable ever since — until Ben collapsed from dysplasia. His passion had been chasing sticks; Tanjy's was chasing cats. Yet when Tanjy, who lay grieving for Ben, spied that cat, he sprang up and ran to welcome it! He actually began to lick its face before settling down beside it. And Goldie, as we promptly named the newcomer, stretched and yawned luxuriously, as if enjoying his advances. I will always believe that God sent that golden cat that almost *looked* like Ben to comfort Tanjy in his loss.

It wasn't the same, however, just as nothing could ever be the same for me after losing George. And my heart went out to Tanjy, as I heard that plaintive barking at the window. The poor little guy must have been doubly bereft, for he had lost not only his master, but also Ben, his life's dearest companion.

We four had become a little family. Now it was only the three of us, counting Goldie, and we needed each other. And although I took them a different route, we walked as long as we could in the descending darkness, if only to postpone the desolate hours ahead. But it had turned so cold, this bitter winter of my darling's death: blizzards and ice storms that were severe for Pittsburgh, as if the whole world had frozen and was determined to freeze us with it, forever ice-bound and alone.

Stubbornly some nights I resisted, bundling up in boots and scarf and mittens, and took Tanjy anyway, slipping and skidding across the white brilliance in the dusk. But we couldn't go far; his little legs were so short I sometimes had to carry him. And it wasn't safe with this ice and brutal cold. Even so, the escape was just what we needed.

Panting, flesh stinging, yet refreshed by the battle, I would bring him in, dry him off, and let him snooze beside the gas log fire until it was time to go upstairs and flop down beside my bed, where the cat would already be sleeping. We had always slept with our dogs, and now I wanted to have those warm, furry little bodies beside me. It wasn't quite so lonely. It even made me feel safer.

Meanwhile, I would turn on the television set in the kitchen and poke around, opening and closing cupboards, trying to decide what to have for supper. It didn't matter anymore what or where I ate. Or if I ate at all, except to keep me alive. Usually something in the refrigerator — whatever I could find, a bowl of soup or a TV dinner, although I sometimes cooked a whole meal to make it last longer and shorten the evening.

But there were times, even after I'd gone to all that trouble, when I would push the plate aside, bury my face in my folded arms, and cry.

It was on such an evening, after our walk in the snow, that a marvelous thing began.

I could feel a hand on my shoulder, patting it as if to comfort me. Then the same hand gripping my fingers, squeezing them over and over: 1-4-3,

1-4-3, our private code for "I'm thinking of you, I love you," representing the number of letters in the words "I love you." Startled, I realized they were my own fingers, locked together so tightly I couldn't pull them apart! They had moved of their own volition. And suddenly I *knew* that George was with me. I could feel his presence in the room.

Chapter Four

THE CONVERSATIONS

IT'S TRUE, IT'S TRUE!

Thank you, dear God,

for answering my prayers for discernment.

Now I can be sure.

It's true, it's true!

My husband is still by my side.

The messages I've been receiving from him

are so beautiful and reassuring,

I know this has to be your will.

To doubt this would be like doubting *you!*

"*G*EORGE, GEORGE!" I cried softly, awed and thrilled, yet a part of me strangely calm. Actually I was more relieved at this joyful confirmation than surprised. For I had talked to him ever since his death, aloud or in my head, praying and believing that he heard and that sometime, somehow he would answer. George would find a way, if anybody could. And as I sat there breathless, daring to hope, the miracle of his presence was revealed.

He spoke to me. I could hear his voice clearly — that rich familiar baritone with its musical cadences, like no other voice I had ever heard. It was not audible to my ears, but I recognized it at once. There was no doubt whatever.

Quickly I freed my fingers and from instinct and habit reached for the pen and pad I kept on every table to take down in shorthand the wonderful things he said. I had done this almost every day of our lives together. I had been working on a book about us. As both wife and writer I wanted to make people realize how sweet marriage can be at *any* age. But even more important, I wanted them to have their own marriages sweetened, their lives enriched, and their faith enhanced by George's beautiful philosophy.

But compared to what I was hearing tonight, all else paled. I knew that now as never before it was important to capture and share the things God was letting him tell me. And this is what he said:

"Marjorie, Marjorie...oh, my dearest, cry if it helps, but please don't worry. I am still by your side. I love you so much. We love *each other* so much. And when the bonds of love on earth are strong, they can't be broken, even by death....

"The George who loved you will always be with you. I am with you now, I can see you there in the kitchen, with those tears running down your face as you write, wondering if this is true. You aren't imagining this, honey, *it is true.* I am with you. I was with you and Tanjy tonight, struggling through all that ice and snow. But enjoying it, almost having fun until it got so cold.

"I was happy for you; you were still radiant when you came in. But I could feel your loneliness and grief coming on again. And when you got your poor little supper ready, and then couldn't eat it, I had to try to comfort you. I felt the warmth of your shoulder when I touched it, and your fingers gripping mine so tight you could hardly let go.

"Oh, Marjorie, please dear, whenever you're sad, remember the vow we took at our wedding: 'I will never leave thee nor forsake thee.' And how we said those words to each other every morning and night, and whenever we lifted a glass. Say them again, they will make you feel better. Because I want you to know *you have not been forsaken,* I will never leave thee!"

For a few moments there was silence. Breathless, I waited, overjoyed, Thank God, thank God! Yet still with that curious sense of peace and calm and reassurance.

"Yes, I am also in heaven, just as Jesus promised us we would be if we loved him. And oh, Marj, it *is* so beautiful! Beyond description or imagination. Beyond anything you and I ever saw on our travels: all those castles and cathedrals, all the mountains and lakes and seas. The most fabulous places on earth can't compare. And I will hold your hand and be with you when it's time for you to see it. Because we will be together here forever."

Again there was a brief silence, while my heart

45

raced, eager for more, yet with that curious calm. And what George said next was the most thrilling and comforting of all.

"Marjorie, my dearest, don't let your heart be troubled, you have nothing to be concerned about. God wants all his children to be happy. He does not limit the soul — a soul has more than one dimension. *The George who loved you,*" he repeated, "will be here for you, I promise. And our two souls will never be parted again."

Faint with relief, I had dropped the pen and was sobbing for joy as I heard his final words — sung softly just as he always sang or spoke them to me at bedtime: "Goodnight, sweetheart. *Goodnight!*"

The George who loved you ... The soul is not limited to one dimension. ... I hugged those words to my heart all night. He hadn't been specific. That wasn't necessary; I was sure I knew what he meant. And although I didn't completely understand, I felt a sweet acceptance. My mind with its troubled probings was at rest.

And in later conversations, George made it even clearer. For to my enormous hope and thanksgiving, these conversations continued for several days, the rest of that week, usually in the early evening, right after dinner.

I began to look forward to them, and I believe Tanjy did too. He would start his frantic barking, then scurry around my legs before dropping at my feet, head cocked, emitting a faint contented rumbling, as if in welcome. Or so it seemed.

And once more I would feel my husband's presence. The hand on my shoulder or lightly touching my hair. And my own fingers locking to give our familiar signal, before pulling away to record his message. What follows are the essence of those messages, in no special order, as much as I could capture and transcribe later. Sometimes I paused to cry, sometimes to laugh, thinking what his family would say if they knew: "Well, that's Dad, all right! Never could shut him up. But at least he was never boring."

Sometimes the revelations were coming so fast that my hand simply flew across the page, leaving only a trail of flourishes, swoops, and swirls in a kind of heavenly shorthand that only an angel could interpret. Or maybe it was just my own exuberant spirit having a heavenly dance with George. We both loved to dance; for us it was as thrilling as making love.

But most of the time my hands and my heart behaved as I listened, however awed:

"Honey, please don't grieve. I am still by your side, and I must tell you again: It's true, it's true! And so beautiful, beyond human comprehension. And more — we are being fulfilled in all that we were meant to be on earth, every good thing we longed to do. Because we're not idle in this state of bliss, but enjoying the bliss of accomplishment. Your father with his inventions. Your mother with her own literary talents — so happy knowing they are bearing such fruits in you. Nothing is ever wasted. It is all being sent to help people on earth.

"So please don't be troubled about your book. It's God's book too, remember, and he will not let it fail. Be patient, have faith, you will have time to finish it, and it will be well received. And you will continue to achieve when we are together again. The two of us just as we were when we met, knowing instantly that we belonged to each other forever. One final union that has nothing to do with the people we were before.... Those couples were separate entities, with different lives to lead. Your book *Second Wife, Second Life* is well-named. To marry a second time, especially at our age, *is* to begin a second life.

"We were not meant to meet earlier. We had to grow as people. We had to grow as souls. We weren't ready for each other. We were both committed, and on earth the love between husband and wife has to be exclusive. There is room for only one true love at a time. Nature made us so, and that is God's way. But in eternity there are different dimensions of the soul.

"Never mind where the other man, the George you never knew, is now. That too is eternal, and has to be fulfilled. But you and I, the great love that we created is immortal. God brought us together and made it so. God planned it that way from the beginning. We were soulmates, destined to become one.... All this will become clear to you sometime.

"Try not to hurt too much. You have many years to be happy and accomplish the things the Lord wants you to. And when you come to join me he will use both of us to accomplish even more.

"As I've said before, and promise you now — the George you knew will always be with you, Marjorie, my final love for all eternity...."

That was all for several months, until once again my life would change.

Chapter Five

DECISIONS

DECISIONS

Please help me make the right decisions, Lord:

Whether to go or stay.

Help me to remember that whatever I choose,

wherever I go,

it will be the rest of my life without George.

And once that choice is made,

help me never to regret it.

God, you in your great wisdom,

know what's best for me —

and for the work you have given me to do.

Let this be *your* choice for me.

Use me wherever you need me.

And give me the strength and will power

not to waste my life in grieving

for the one I have lost,

but rather rejoicing in the challenge

of all that I still can do for others —

and so for you.

T WAS EASIER after that. Although I still chatted away with George aloud or in my head, I somehow knew those important messages from him could not continue. I realized they were a gift from God, sent only to comfort and sustain my faith during those first agonizing days without him. I must get on with my life. As George had said, I still had much work to do. There were still so many people I could help and encourage with my writing.

Two new books were almost finished. Not only "our book," the one I'd been worrying about, but another one, *Writing Articles from the Heart,* under contract to *Writers Digest* (a revised, updated version of one of my previous titles published by *The Writer*). There were also speaking dates and other commitments that don't take a holiday, no matter what happens.

Thank God for them! My time had been so fractured these past few years, inching along on these projects, as George insisted, even when I was caring for him. Now I could give them my full attention. So I stopped expecting those miracle messages that had been coming each evening. And strangely, even Tanjy did too. He no longer kept his anxious vigil at the window. Instead, he would lie moping beside the cat. Or to my alarm, he would disappear. He got away almost every time the door was open, and I would have to hunt for him. Once he got clear down to the schoolhouse; once he was almost hit by a car. I was afraid he was losing his hearing.

Finally, in desperation, I called George's family to ask if I shouldn't put him to sleep. "The poor little thing is so miserable — he misses Ben and your dad so much."

"Of course," they assured me, "and it's hard on you too. One of us will be over in the morning to take him to the vet."

But I told them no, I could do it myself, "The way we did with Ben, remember?" Both dogs had been in the family so long it seemed cruel to send either one off to die with strangers. "I still have a lot of those sleeping pills your father gave him. And I'll sit with Tanjy and talk to him and tell him how much we love him until he falls asleep, just as we did with Ben."

"Okay, if you think you're up to it," young

Dr. George agreed. "But call me if you need any help. And of course I'll come later to bury him."

⁏

It wasn't as easy as I thought. I decided to put it off until evening, when I could feed him one last supper. Making sure I had all his favorite foods. Unlike Ben, Tanjy was not a big eater — actually a little finicky about what he ate. But that night his appetite seemed voracious; he devoured everything as if he might never eat again. And as the time approached for the fatal pills, I almost lost my nerve. Feeling scared and sad and guilty, I tried to comfort him as I explained: "Now honey, I'm going to give you some pills that will make you go to sleep for a long time. But when you wake up I'll bet you'll be in a beautiful place where you'll even see Daddy and Ben again!"

If he suspected my treachery, he gave no sign. That dog ate two large chicken legs, three slices of baloney, a piece of ham, and a piece of cake before I stopped him, afraid he might explode! Gee, then I wouldn't have to give him anything, I thought, not knowing whether to laugh or cry.

So I pried his mouth open and poured in the pills. Then I sat with him, sobbing and cuddling him and making more foolish promises as he began to drowse. And when I was sure he was sound asleep, I signed him with the cross, as my George would, and staggered upstairs to take one of the pills myself.... Twice I crept back down in the night to check on him — still sleeping peacefully, to my surprise.

And to my astonishment, his bark woke me up in the morning! He was wagging his tail at the bottom of the steps, frantic to go out. So I took him, and brought him in for a generous breakfast, and more pills — thinking I must not have given him enough. Evidently he didn't *want* to die, I realized, stricken. Although groggy, he gazed at me so pathetically, as if begging for another reprieve.

This went on most of the day. Finally, I called George for help, as he'd said to do if necessary, and described what had happened.

"Oh, Marj, no — you shouldn't have fed him!" he exclaimed. "Didn't you know? I should have warned you. Those pills will only work on an empty stomach. Now it's gone so far he can't live much longer anyway; but I'll come over and give him a shot to put him out of his misery."

He came within the hour, carrying the familiar black bag that reminded me of his father, and with the shovel he used so recently to dig the grave for Ben. Years ago the family had gotten permission from the health department to bury its many pets in their huge yard just beyond the garden. And there he carried Tanjy to sleep beside his friend.

So now I was alone again. Except for Goldie, who would purr and entwine my legs so lovingly, as she had done with George and even Tanjy. All three of them gone now — first Ben, then George, and now Tanjy, who hadn't wanted to go, it hurt to remember. I was only trying to help him, but now I understood. Life is so precious to every living thing, how can we bear to leave it? Yet time keeps running out for all of us. And there are times when we must choose what is best for the life remaining. Tanjy was actually the last link of my own little family here with George. Like him, I didn't want to leave, but I wondered if I should stay.

George had given me life estate in both properties, that is, the right to use the properties as long as I live — not only this big beautiful home, but also the lovely cottage on Lake Erie. But what did that matter without him? Nothing would ever be the same. This house still ached with his presence. Everything he'd touched was so dear to me.

There were the few clothes I'd left in his closet after giving the rest away: the suit he'd worn at our wedding, and one of the blue lab coats that matched his eyes, his big cowboy hat that he liked to doff with a flourish and a booming, "Howdy, Miss Elly!" Our matching fisherman's caps that he'd bought on our trip to Greece....

There were also his mountains of books, mostly medicine, poetry, philosophy, and religion, as well as literally thousands of jokes, cartoons and clippings. Plus there were nearly eleven years of his daily notes and love letters. I had kept every one, sometimes dated but in no special order in the sacks, and I still read one aloud every night, as I had always done at bedtime. "Your note, your note!" George would proclaim if I forgot, and he always sat listening with the pride and joy of a little boy. Now all this was over, and it hurt even as it comforted me.

"Why am I *staying?*" I wondered. My own children lived far away. And nice as people were, I had almost no friends in Pittsburgh. I had been so busy with my writing and so fulfilled just being with George. I hadn't joined the Press Club or even the doctors' wives in the Medical Auxiliary. And although George wouldn't have protested, I knew it pleased him. He and his first wife seldom socialized. Actually, they were very exclusive, living only for each other and their family.

This had troubled me at first. It was such a far cry from my life in Washington, where my husband was district manager for Carrier Corporation, and I was a columnist on the *Washington Star.* Joining clubs, making friends, giving and going to parties was a part of our jobs. And we enjoyed it. It was an escape from our problems, and some of those friends became very dear to us. We needed them, because as a couple we were simply not that close.

So it wasn't hard for George to convince me, "If two people really love each other the way we do, why waste time with a lot of other people who don't mean a thing? Make the most of every minute you can have together. And remember you and I got a late start, honey. As I've said so often, we haven't *got* that much time!"

But now that my only reason for being here was over, I realized I should make some plans for the future. Maybe I should go back to Virginia, to the home I had left to marry him nearly eleven years before. The house was still waiting there on the lake where he found me — actually two houses side by side on a peninsula completely surrounded by water. We had married in such a hurry there hadn't been time to dispose of the property, and George urged me not to anyway.

He had fallen in love with it too. "It's so beautiful here; we could come back for holidays with your children."

George and I did go there several times a year. And always for Christmas, a day which his own family dedicated to the memory of their mother.

And now my children were urging me to consider moving back. "Most of us will be closer and as you know, Mother, there's plenty of room."

The smaller house had begun as a log-cabin hideaway where we could fish and swim. But we'd all enjoyed it so much, we worked very hard to restore, rebuild, and enlarge it into a rustic year-round country home. And when the larger house next door came up for sale, we had bought that too, for family gatherings and to be available to any of the family who ever needed it. And with four offspring coming and going, between jobs or marriages or just regrouping, it was never idle. At the moment my older daughter and her husband, a semi-retired Hollywood filmmaker, were living in "the big house," as we called it.

But it was too early to make such a decision. George had died in early January, only four months before. And I was too busy meeting deadlines on my books. Editing was in progress on both of them. There was the usual flurry of revisions and phone calls and letters to be exchanged. But I was thankful for it. It was like a drug, easing the incessant pain of missing George. And in September I'd be flying to New York to deliver my traditional closing speech, "Make the Most of Your Talent," for the *Guideposts* Writers Conference.

This was always an inspiring task. The audience featured the fifteen winners of a *Guideposts* writing contest, whose manuscripts had been chosen out of at least three thousand submissions. Their prize was this trip to New York for a week of training by the *Guideposts* editors and staff — concluding with my usual pep talk to spur them on.

George had always enjoyed going with me. He was a great admirer of Norman Vincent Peale. And he would never forget the night Dr. Peale gave me a flattering introduction followed by, "And that guy with her is no slouch either!" George bragged about that compliment the rest of his life.

It would be my first year without him since our marriage. They knew it would hard for me and weren't sure I would be able to come. But "Yes, oh yes!" I told them. "Although there's still so much to be done and my future is very uncertain, you're all so dear to me I need you now more than ever."

Chapter Six

COMING HOME

THE ACCIDENT: SLOW ME DOWN

Slow me down, Lord.

Please don't let me go on

doing everything so fast.

If I'd listened to George's warnings about it

this accident wouldn't have happened!

But it did happen, Lord,

and at the time I didn't understand.

I take such good care of my body,

and had never broken a bone in my life before.

Wasn't it enough

that my heart was already breaking?

How could you *let* this happen?

But now I realize what a blessing it was.

That for those who love the Lord,

all things do work together for good.

This accident has solved the problem

of whether to go or stay.

Through it

you have made my decision for me....

(But please keep on trying to slow me down!)

THE CHANGE was just what I needed. These *Guideposts* Writers Conferences have a special mystique of their own, a quality of such faith and hope and enthusiasm it's like a fresh baptism of the Spirit! For me that force was especially strong this year. Never have I felt more comforted or truly admired and loved.

I flew home counting my blessings, in a state of near euphoria. Since I hadn't been sure about my schedule, there was nobody to meet my plane. So I grabbed a taxi, and the minute we arrived, I raced upstairs to rest and savor this feeling. I had barely settled down, however, when the doorbell rang below. Oh, golly, I'd forgotten — it must be our neighbor, Margaret Fedor, bringing back the cat.

"Be right down!" I yelled, although I knew she couldn't hear me, and jumped off the bed at the end of that thirty-foot room and ran.

George was always warning me to be more careful. "Try not to do everything so fast, honey. You could fall and get seriously hurt." But I hadn't paid attention. And it didn't occur to me until too late.

Just before reaching the stairs, I whirled to pick up my glasses and skidded. Suddenly I had the ghastly feeling of feet flying into the air and my body crash-landing on a hip!

Shocked and protesting (this *couldn't* be happening to me!) I lay screaming for a moment. Then in mortal agony, I squirmed and clawed my way for at least half an hour to get back to the bed and grope for the phone, which fell into my lap.

Young George was home, thank God. "Don't move!" he ordered. "I'll call the ambulance." Meanwhile, he also called the best orthopedic surgeon he knew, Dr. Stephen Theis, who was away on vacation. But that dear man promised to fly right back and operate in the morning.

Still on the floor, I phoned my daughter Mickie, in Virginia, to let the family know. Her brother Mallory drove all night to be with me. His sisters followed the next day. All four of them — two sons and two daughters — began taking turns to see me through this ordeal, as they had done when my George was so ill. And his own children couldn't have been more helpful and loving.

I was in excellent shape, thanks to a lot of swimming and dancing, and made a remarkable recovery: only a week in the hospital; two weeks of physical therapy from lovely young women who came to our home; only a week of using a walker, and I didn't even need a cane.

Nonetheless, I had to be careful. And on one issue we all agreed. "Mother, it simply isn't safe for you to live in that big house alone."

Thus was my future settled. As soon as Dr. Theis gave his consent, I would come home! Immediately the packing and planning began. George and I had married so fast I had brought very little with me: mostly clothes and personal things, and of course my writing equipment. His house was already so abundantly furnished. I resolved to take little more back with me when I left — only the things we had given each other or acquired on our travels and a few pieces of furniture we had bought for ourselves. Even so, quite a lot can accumulate in nearly eleven years. But not enough to hire professional movers, my sons decided. They would simply rent a big U-Haul van, which Mallory would tow behind his truck.

The day before we were to leave, when the van

was almost loaded, Mallory opened a closet and discovered the huge piles of sacks filled with George's love notes and letters — sometimes two or three a day. In all those years I'd never thrown one away. "Oh, Mother," he groaned, "I'm so sorry I forgot these! What'll we do about them?" He paused to study my anxious face. "You really want them, don't you?" And as I nodded meekly, "Okay, we'll *make* room for them in the van!" And that night, remembering that I always read something from George at bedtime, he set one sack beside my bed.

It had been a sweet but exhausting day. Saying goodbye to neighbors and others who came bearing gifts and offers to help...Realizing this would be my last night in our beautiful home, where I would always be loved to sleep in my husband's arms.

I hurried my bath and got to bed as soon as I could. There I opened the sack and reached blindly in. And what I drew out was so astonishing I caught my breath and wept in sheer ecstasy as I read:

Oh my Darling — Entreat me never to leave thee or forsake thee nor to return from following after thee; for whither thou goest I too will

go; and where thou lodgest I will lodge, and
thy people (Mark, Mallory and Judy, Mickie
and Stan, Melanie and Haris, Gwen, Harold,
etc.) shall be my people and thy God my God.
Where thou diest (Air, Land or Sea) I will also
die; and there I will be buried; the Lord do so
to me and more also, if aught but death parts
thee and me.

RUTH TO NAOMI
GEORGE TO MARJORIE

For a moment I was too enthralled to speak. But this was so significant, almost incredible, I simply had to share it. Still weeping I ran down the hall, calling out to Mallory and his wife, Judy, and to Melanie, whose room was next to theirs. They too were amazed and puzzled.

"Mother, have you ever read this before?" they asked.

"Only in the Bible," I told them. "But never George's version, written in his own hand!"

Oh my darling — Entreat me never to leave thee or forsake thee nor to return from following after thee; for whither thou goest I too will go; and where thou lodgest I will lodge; thy people (MARY, MALLORY, Mickey & Stan, melanie & harris, Gwen, Harold etc) shall be my people and thy God, my God. Where thou diest (Air, Land or Sea) I will also die; and there I will be buried; the Lord do so to me and more also, if aught but death parts thee and me. Ruth to Naomi
George to Marjorie

It's a long trip from Pittsburgh to Manassas, Virginia, and usually takes about eight hours. This time it would take even longer, following a loaded van. (Judy and Mallory had driven up together; I would ride with them.)

Knowing we wanted to get an early start, Diane had said not to worry about breakfast; she'd bring it over. She's a fabulous cook, and what a farewell feast it was, including a huge fruit platter, tiny sausages, fresh croutons, and her specialty, an omelet that is pure ambrosia.

There was some laughing and kidding as we ate, but Diane and I were also fighting tears. And when it was time to say goodbye, we both broke down. "Oh, Marj," she said, "it was so hard losing my mother, then Dad. I never thought I could feel so bad again — or worse. But now — to lose you *too!*"

"Honey, we're both *alive*," I told her. "This isn't final; we will see each other again."

"But you'll be so far away, it will never be the same."

"No," I had to admit. "Things can never be the same for any of us. Nothing lasts forever. But we can thank God for the wonderful times we've had.

75

And I can promise you this: you *will* see your mother and father again, and we'll all be together in heaven." At that point I decided to show her the letter. I hadn't been quite sure how she'd take it. But she too read it in awed amazement, then gazed at me intently. "That's no coincidence, Marj. That's *Dad!* The most incredible man I ever met. I'm proud to be his daughter. Now *git!*"

Laughing, I climbed into the car, feeling somehow freed and confirmed by her blessing.

It was a glorious sunny day, and my heart was at peace as we drove the familiar route George and I had taken so often. To quote Ann Morrow Lindbergh, I believe: "Nothing is so exhausting as indecision." Now that part was settled; the Lord had decided for me. I was filled with a joyful sense of anticipation. It was like a new beginning, almost starting over — going back to the place where the beautiful story of my life with George began. And he was going with me! The evidence was in my pocket.

The trip went surprisingly fast, as we laughed and talked and cheered Mallory and his lumbering cargo on. We stopped for lunch and to rest and enjoy the sandwiches and snacks Diane had provided in case we got hungry. Even so, it was after dark when our little caravan arrived at Manassas and started down the long bumpy road to Lake Jackson.

The house was bright with lighted candles in every window, balloons, and a huge sign that read: MOTHER, WELCOME HOME! Those who had waited for us were beaming in the doorway or running to meet us: Mickie and Stan, Mark and his daughter, Kathy, Melanie's husband, Haris, their children, Alexi and Adam. It was so festive and sweet I laughed and cried.

We were exhausted, of course, and after a lot of hugging and kissing and coffee, we were eager to get to bed. But meanwhile, the men were unloading our bags, and Mallory a few sacks of my precious letters. And when I had finished my bath and went into my room, I found one sack standing beside my bed, as usual. Touched and pleased, I untied it and reached in, plucking only two papers which were stuck together at the top,

The first one said:

> *Dearest Marjorie*
> *Welcome Back!*
> *I Missed You*
> *Always*
> *Love*
> *George.*

The second one said simply:

> *Dear Marjorie*
> *I'm very*
> *happy you arrived*
> *safely home.*

Dearest Marjorie
Welcome
Back
I Missed
You Always
Love
Georgie

Dear Marjorie
I'm very
happy you arrived
safely home

Chapter Seven

ON THE ROAD AGAIN

ALL THESE COMMITMENTS

Oh, God, dear God, thank you

for all these activities and commitments

that will keep me from grieving for George.

But part of me is *scared!*

I'm afraid I've taken on too much.

All this speaking and traveling without him

(which I didn't mind doing alone

before we met).

But now, but now,

after having him go with me so long,

it hurts, it hurts!

But I've given my word,

and somehow, some way,

I must find the courage and strength

to get through it.

Hold me up a little longer, Lord,

don't let me break down!

If I fail this I'll be failing *him*,

and my book about our beautiful marriage.

That's why I wrote it —

to share this wonderful man with the world.

His philosophy, his humor,

his thrilling convictions about you, Lord,

and life and death and love.

Now please get me through

all of these commitments

without going to pieces before I get back!

*T*HREE OF THE HARDEST experiences of life, it's been said, are a personal injury, a death in the family, having to move. I returned to my "new life" in Manassas, Virginia, shaken by all three.

The first few months were a storm of activity, unpacking things, storing things, and deciding *where* to put *what* in space that now seemed so limited compared to the roomy office I had just left behind.

My family had worked like tigers to prepare for my return. Despite my quick recovery, I still had to be careful about the hip. It was too soon for me to go up and down stairs to my spacious workshop on the lower floor beside the lake. Their father had built it for me when we first came here. With my habit of running, it might even be dangerous, they worried. So they had chosen the long glassed-in porch beside the living room for my study and had managed to cram in most of my writing equipment — desks, chairs, typewriter, word processor, and files.

Thank God for these loving, caring grown children! Sometimes I was almost overwhelmed with their kindness, half-dismayed, half-amused to remember that each one had been a surprise we thought we couldn't afford, or weren't sure we wanted to at the time, yet loved so desperately the minute they were in our arms. And despite many problems, every one of them had proved to be such a blessing — especially whenever I needed them, and I needed them now, as never before.

I also thanked God for my work, which kept me so madly busy I literally didn't have time or strength to grieve. Both books were being published that spring, which is very unusual, and were even released on the same April day. I would be speaking, autographing, and often traveling, well beyond the rest of the year.

My whole being still longed for George, but his spirit went with me. I knew he was amused as well as pleased to hear me quoting the wonderful things he had said in "our book" about him. And night after night, wherever I was, I could feel my fingers locking to receive the brisk little squeezes saying, "1-4-3, 1-4-3" (his secret code for "I love you"). Then I would read one of his romantic, flattering, but always funny notes, which made me laugh and comforted me to sleep.

Even so, I didn't feel secure enough physically or emotionally to undertake another promotion tour. These tours, which look glamorous, are actually very hard work — traveling to different cities day after day, for interviews, book signings, and sometimes a speech. I'd taken many of them by myself, or accompanied by a salesman, and always came home exhilarated but exhausted. It was easier after marrying George, because he always went with me. Together we'd flown coast to coast for each of my last three books. And every trip was like another honeymoon. He was such a handsome, entertaining, and loving escort I couldn't bear the thought of taking such a trip again without him.

And what if I *broke down* someplace?

But I did accomplish a lot in or near Washington: at churches, bookstores, libraries, the Press Club, and, as the Christmas season approached, hospital bazaars. At one event, feeling like the President, I lighted a huge Christmas tree!

And wherever I went, a wonderful thing began to happen. I felt a great surge of love surrounding me.

People were reaching out to me, not only with their books to be signed, but their *hearts,* to squeeze my hand or to hug me, some of them with tears in their eyes as they spoke of their own lost loved ones. And over and over they thanked me for all the books of prayers I'd written. "You'll never know how much you've helped me. Please call me if I can ever do anything for you...."

None of them realized how much this unexpected outpouring was already doing for me. I'd heard these same words before and read them often in fan mail, but this time was somehow different. Just being *alone* makes everything different. We had suddenly changed roles; now my readers were comforting *me!*

I started the New Year by flying to my home town, Storm Lake, Iowa, to speak for "Salute to Women," an annual event sponsored by the Chamber of Commerce to honor its own women of achievement. The auditorium was packed with people from miles around to "salute" these wonderful women. I was proud to be in their company and so grateful for another chance to "come home again," now that George was gone. Although I had been back many times before, this visit had tremendous new significance for me. So many of my family and even my friends were also gone; and with life flying by so fast for all of us, who knew how many more homecomings we would have?

It was a very joyful, healing, and nostalgic week: driving those familiar streets with my older brother, Harold; seeing the parks, and the beautiful lake where I learned to swim almost as soon as I could walk, and the wonderful old houses where life actually began for the Sam Holmes family. Even the house where our parents met was still standing.

Here I had dreamed of becoming a writer, scribbling away at a little desk my Grandpa Griffith had made for me. Here was the high school where I graduated. And Buena Vista College, where a remarkable teacher named Dewey Deal, who had already encouraged me in junior high, had become head of the English department. And there at "B.V." she confirmed that dream by the words she wrote on a paper, which I framed and still have hanging over my desk: "Marjorie, Marjorie, you *must* make the most of your talent. I know that *if you want to badly enough,* you can write beautiful things for people who crave beautiful things. *There is a duty!*"

And now those memories were even more significant, because the last time I had come back, George had been with me. It was his first trip to Iowa, the year we had been invited to lead the parade on the Fourth of July. And oh, how he had enjoyed it — the music, the marching, and waving exuberantly to the crowds from that open car! It was so *like him,* I laughed as I remembered. It's one of my tenderest memories of our marriage.

And I will never stop thanking God for giving him that opportunity to see where I had come from and to share this thrilling experience before he had to lose his legs, and it would have been too late.

Although a book tour was out, I returned home feeling so much better that I was happy to go when my publishers wanted to send me to the CBA —

the Christian Booksellers Convention in Atlanta. Like the *Guideposts* Writers Conference, it's always rejuvenating, swarming with editors, writers, and publishers from all over the world. Some of them had become very good friends over the years, among them, bestselling Hollywood author Roger Elwood and Colonel Houston Ellis, of the Salvation Army, who took turns seeing that I got to the right places on time and shepherding me to meals. That in itself made the whole trip worthwhile.

I think the one thing a widow misses most is no longer having a male escort, especially if you've been married most of your adult life. There is something so strong and protective about a man, even the little courtesies like opening the door for you, seating you at a table, giving your order to a waiter. And the mere physical presence of a kind and decent man who's responsible for you is comforting and reassuring.

But the very first morning, returning from breakfast with Houston, as I scurried up the curved steps of the Peachtree Hotel, I tripped and landed on my right wrist — with books to sign tomorrow! Swearing him to secrecy, I begged him not to call the emergency room, but to order ice and a pain killer, which might be all I needed.

Praying desperately, I rested all afternoon. By evening, the arm was black to the elbow. But that night, careful to wear long sleeves, I was Roger's guest at a big Word Books publishing party. Roger also promised not to tell my editor, Mike Iannazzi. I was scared he might think, "Dumb author, always breaking something!" and want to throw me out. But my prayers were answered. The next day I signed six hundred books at the Doubleday booth and didn't tell Mike until we were on our way to the airport. Actually he was very sweet, urging me to get an X-ray, which I did when I got home. And it proved I had broken only one small bone in the wrist.

Please Note: Despite my hip replacement, I can still do everything I used to, except jump on my trampoline and try to kick the ceiling. But I *am* dumb enough to do everything too fast without watching where I'm going!

I also treated myself to a working holiday, greeting old friends and signing books at the National Federation of Press Women's convention in Kansas City. Here again to my surprise, I felt that remarkable surge of love and true appreciation for my work that I'm sure helped me as much, or even more, than I had helped them others. Two weeks later I was off to speak for the annual Seminar for Seniors, in Florence, South Carolina, where my son lives, and I felt the same support.

But there were two more places arranged for earlier that I knew I must not miss, but secretly dreaded: Pittsburgh, the very heart and soul of my life with George, and our summer home at Portland Bay on Lake Erie. Leaving had been hard enough; I feared returning would be worse, because it would be so final.

Diane had invited me to stay with them when I came. She and her new husband, Colin, now lived in the big Tudor house where she had grown up and her father and I had been so happy. Colin is a builder; they had remodeled everything, from the landscaping to the entire interior — which was better for them and probably for me during my stay. Diane gave a lovely party for me the night I arrived — mostly family and neighbors. But my schedule was so crowded and she gets to her labs at the hospital so early, I actually saw very little of them.

Even so, she had my breakfast ready for the microwave every morning, gave me the biggest rosebud I ever saw to wear to the autographings (four in the next four days, plus interviews), and came to most of them. All the interviews were very successful, thank God. (I'd had the ghastly nightmare that most authors have sometimes: of sitting alone at a table with your books, but *nobody* comes to buy them!)

My close friend, Hope Hathaway, arrived with a big delegation from her home at nearby Carmichaels. George's granddaughter Pam brought her Christian Nurses group. Another granddaughter, Debbie, and her fiancé didn't miss a one. There were also George's patients. And friends and followers I didn't know I *had!* I was so relieved I almost wept and came home rejoicing.

Part of my secret dread about returning was again that I might break down or somehow fail George and his family here where he had been a beloved physician for so long.

⌒

The next trip was just as hard to face emotionally: our Paradise on Lake Erie, to sign books and get the last of my things from the cottage.

It's a ten-hour drive. My girls persuaded me to fly to Jamestown, New York, while one of them would follow in Melanie's van. Our closest friend there, Mary Downs, met my plane and "took me home again." Mickie arrived that night. The next morning we had barely started packing when the neighbors who had welcomed me so warmly as a bride began to arrive with food, invitations — and strong arms to help load the van for my departure.

Here too I had so much office equipment, we had thought we might have to ship some things. But by some miracle, as at home, those precious people got my books, desk, copier, typewriter, and three filing cabinets into that van! (I'd given away my big, old-fashioned extra word processor.)

And they loyally flocked to the autographing

party at The Book Nook, a favorite store. Wonderful publicity and a sellout crowd, ... several dinner parties, walks on the beach, one last swim, a final tour of the lush green yard and the point, where an ancient tree still clings to its perch above the water — roots dangling, as they have for years, refusing to crash and fall like the others.

Goodbye, old tree, hang on as long as you can. Then lock up and try not to cry as you drive away....

And I *didn't* cry until after we got home the next day.

Chapter Eight

WHAT I HAVE LEARNED
FROM GRIEF

It's No Disgrace to Cry

Thank you, dear God,

for the healing power of expressing our grief.

You had a reason for giving us this release.

I don't have to fight it any more,

or be ashamed to cry.

I think of the beautiful story in the Bible,

what your own son did

when told of the death

of his best friend, Lazarus,

and hurried to the tomb:

Jesus wept.

HAT DAY the floodgates opened, and the tears I'd repressed so long wouldn't stop. I didn't want them to. I was tired, so unutterably tired, and it was such a relief to be home again where I was free to let go and express the true depths of sorrow I had only been postponing. Even though George was still by my side in spirit, I knew this was necessary to my healing and, even more important, to my *understanding* of what other people go through.

I had read several times that experts say there are three stages of grief. But I couldn't remember what they were and had no idea which stage I might be in. Only that much as it hurt, it must be experienced.

As I told my daughters when they tried to comfort me: words don't help, reasoning doesn't help. The people who love us do their best, and we appreciate them. But such pain is a private thing. Right now I, at least, was on a lonely journey of the soul seeking its mate. No one else could come with me. And only one person could help me — the very mate I sought. But that must await its hour.

Meanwhile, I discovered that sorrow is an entity of its own, almost a separate presence, a stranger

uninvited that has slipped into the vacant rooms of
your being and lives there day and night in gentle
silence, but strong and ready to support you. Don't
deplore it or fight it; it is not an enemy but a friend
who has a lot to teach you. It is enriching, broad-
ening, deepening, adding to your life's experience. I
had to have it to make me whole.

I had written about it before, in good faith, meaning well, thinking I knew; and some readers were
kind enough to say it had helped and to thank me.
But I blush to remember one article, "Don't Hang
On to Heartbreak," wherein I advised people to
throw out the letters and pictures and keepsakes and
get on with their lives. (Good advice if you're young,
as I was then, but not for the age I am now.) Now
it was my turn, and I not only kept all those letters
and keepsakes but framed some of them, along with
the pictures, and made a veritable shrine to George
in the bedroom.

Worse is the memory of trying to console my Aunt
Ada when she lost her husband, Uncle Wayne. A
couple that seemed to go their separate ways, she
was a vivacious, outspoken school teacher; he an
officer in the bank. She was always with Grandma;

he was always on the golf course. I don't remember ever seeing them together in public or even at family gatherings, only at home, where he was usually buried in a newspaper with his pipe while the rest of us talked. Yet when he died she carried on as if the world was coming to an end. "I know, I know," I murmured tritely, on a visit to Storm Lake.

"No, you *don't* know!" she raged. "If you did you wouldn't *be* here without your husband! I'd give everything I own to see Wayne walk through that door right now."

"I'm sorry," I said helplessly. "I know, I know..."

"No, you *don't!*" she repeated, "Not until you've been *through* it!" Then she hung up on me.

And she was right.

I also remember how I had tried to advise and comfort my mother when she lost Dad, my naivete and temerity, however loving, as I urged her to read an esoteric book that claimed death was just an illusion; it didn't really happen; life just changed forms. The soul could emerge and linger, to become a constant companion if you wanted it to enough. "Try to remember that Dad isn't really gone, he's here with us right now, he'll be with you every day of your life."

I'll never forget how she clutched her Bible to her breast and gazed at me so poignantly with her big, pleading eyes. "But oh, *Marj*," she wailed, almost fiercely, *"you miss the body too!"*

Yes, yes, of course, I thought, not really understanding then. Not even completely understanding later when she confided in me that my jovial traveling salesman father had made love to her *every* night he was home or they were together, almost to the night he died.

I had to wait and marry a man like George before I truly understood. George was so *physical,* as well as philosophical. That magnificent body of his — not only making love, but as we swam and dived and danced together, climbed the cliffs at Lake Erie, ran the dogs across the hills. Just to be with him was exhilarating. Oh, how I missed that body!

And those strong, beautiful, healing hands that had examined other bodies every day when he was in practice. He was that rarity, a "hands-on" physician, one who doesn't just ask what's wrong and write a prescription, but discovers it with his searching fingers, if possible, and fixes it by whatever measures it takes.

Oh, to feel those hands exploring my body again, to be held in his arms for even one more dance. To sleep in those arms and wake up beside him.... Dear Mother, Aunt Ada, and all the other women who've ever gone through this, now I can honestly say, "I know, I know!"

That is the state I was in when George himself came to my rescue. It had been a very hard day, with many interruptions and troubles as I tried to get back to my work. I am a compulsive writer and *must* accomplish something every day, no matter what. I'm also my harshest critic, and it *must be right.* But about dinnertime, after the fifth revision of the same page, I gave up and reached for my journal, where I could be honest and try to express my confusion. I carried it onto the patio where I could at least watch the sunset as I wrote:

"Today has somehow been the worst. I am still so tired, I just want to go to sleep and not wake up unless I'm in George's arms. I thank God every morning for another day of life. Outwardly I say the words and a part of me wants to believe them. But the heart and soul of me is somewhere else. For the first time in my life, I almost want it to be over. The entire experience, good and bad, defeat and success. Two good marriages, one great love. Four children. And a wonderful career that allowed me to stay home to enjoy them and raise them myself, and not have them raised by somebody else.... No, it wasn't easy, I had worked very hard to get this far — but yes, oh yes, I've been richly blessed. But now that I'm no longer *needed*...."

I pushed the pen aside and lifted my eyes to enjoy the sunset and be encouraged by its beauty. It was outdoing itself tonight. A breeze had turned the water into a rippling golden mirror, jewelled with explosions of tiny sparkling stars. How George would have loved it!

And suddenly I caught my breath and froze, for I felt his presence. As real as if he stood by my side. Then the touch of a hand on my shoulder and my own fingers instantly flying and locking to receive the familiar signal of little squeezes, 1-4-3, 1-4-3, I love you, I love you. Over and over until I had to pry my hands apart in order to reach for my pen and try to capture his words in shorthand. It was the first message I'd had since coming here — and perhaps the last.

"Oh, Marjorie, my darling, my dearest darling, I *do* see it with you. I am here with you now where I first found you. I see the lake shining in the sun, I see the trees, I see the flowers. I am beside you, my love is with you, my heart is beating with your heart. We are still together, as I've told you before, even though you can't see me, we cannot touch. But our hearts still touch, and will always be one. I am with God and in God and in you now, this minute. I want to hold you, I want to comfort you, but I can only speak to you in silence and with the power of my love. Even in Paradise there are limits; the soul can transcend only so far. It can't materialize, but, oh, how it can continue to love."

To my surprise, I answered him, "But George, I *miss* you so much — *I need you, I need you!* I am only half a person without you! I get so lonely and even scared sometimes, all I can do is pull the covers over my eyes and cry. And I make so many mistakes, I do and say such foolish things sometimes. Sometimes I wonder how anybody can *stand* me, let alone be so nice, as most of them are. Help me, guide me, ask God to give me the wisdom and strength I need to keep my promises, meet my commitments, not fail so many people who look to me for help."

His answer came again, as clearly as before: "Slow down, sweetheart, as I used to warn you, don't take on so much. Your soul is being taught a lesson you don't understand right now. Its meaning will be made clearer as you continue to do the work God meant you for. He never gives you more than you can handle, but you're free to choose. Rest, sweetheart. Try not to work so hard. And remember this: I am yours, I will be yours forever as I promised. And when the Lord decides you have finished your mission on earth, you will find me waiting. You will come to me and we will merge, we will become One. Not one flesh again, but one union of souls. That is the true perfection, the ultimate Paradise, too wonderful to convey in words.

"Get more rest, honey," he said again. "Don't work so hard, be at peace, and trust the Lord to guide you to those on earth who still need what you have to give them."

Chapter Nine

LEARNING TO LIVE WITHOUT YOUR MATE

Second Prayer of Blessing

Dear Lord,

Again I ask you to bless everyone

who is reading this book.

I pray that it is helping them even now.

Above all, that it will deepen their faith

and confirm the knowledge

that true love *is* eternal.

And that when you are ready for us,

we *will* be together forever

with those we have loved so much on earth.

*I*T WAS EASIER after that. As the Bible says, "This too shall pass." I had made my peace with pain. I didn't have to run away from it anymore or live in constant fear of losing control of my emotions. I could stay right where I was and lead a happy, productive life without the actual physical presence of the beloved. Not by trying to forget or put aside our beautiful marriage (that would be impossible), nor dwelling on it unduly, but to rejoice in the rich feast of memories it has given me. And in the sweet marvel of knowing that this love was so strong, a truly great love that really happened, and will never be really over.

Now I want to make the most of it, and if possible help others who are going through a similar loss. And while no two marriages are exactly alike, what follows are some of my own experiences and suggestions old or new that have made my life without a mate still significant and rewarding.

First: *Make use of those precious memories.*

For me, one of them was how George always started his day with affirmation. How he would scribble in that little book I mentioned which he called his A–Z's, listing his blessings alphabetically, and eagerly read aloud to me. I read them to myself now whenever I need a lift. My favorite is the day he described the *S*'s.

"I always enjoy the *S*'s," he wrote. "God gave us so many wonderful, really important things that start with S. Beginning with the *sky,* for instance. The roof of the world, which you can *see* every time you lift your eyes! The sky with its *sunsets* and rainbows and beautiful *stars.* One of those stars the *sun* that heats and lights the world. Why, just thinking about the sun and sky alone is enough to make a man fall on his knees.

"And add to that the *sea,* the very place where life began. In those waters, *salt* waters, were all the elements essential for life...."

On and on he went, praising God for the wonders of *skin, skull, sight,* and even the *soul,* before he got to *silence,* and *sleep,* to which he added merrily, "(Especially with my Marjorie!)" ... Beaming,

George handed me the small leather-bound note-book.

"Take a look at this list for just the last few days," he said. "And I've got a lot more to add before I start on the *T*'s. They're a rich treasury too — see, I've already got one. And each time I find more things to marvel about and thank God for....

"Especially you," he smiled. "I didn't even start writing my A–Z's until I met *Y-O-U!*"

He also left me a priceless legacy of laughter. His jokes and kidding and puns, his quick wit whatever the occasion, even on his way to the operating table, his sheer verve for life and the fun it could be for two people in love, who really enjoy each other and have a sense of humor. I laughed more with George than I'd laughed since I was a child.

He was like a child himself. He even got me to reading the funny papers again, which I hadn't done in years. And I *still* read them (at least his favorites) in memory of him. Which makes me feel better, and is, I believe, even better for the world, because you can't live with someone that sweet and funny without a little bit of it rubbing off on you and making things brighter for other people too.

Second: *Do your best to keep well.*

Nothing is more dreary than a sick or ailing widow; it's so easy to complain and feel sorry for yourself. True, there are a lot of things we simply can't help, accidents and ailments that are beyond our control. But there are also a lot of things we *can* do to avoid them, with or without a doctor. Luckily the doctor I married was just as fanatic as I was about keeping fit through exercise, diet, and vitamin supplements. But even long before George, I'd gotten my start from a wonderful doctor named A. B. Little, who was our neighbor and friend in Takoma Park. Every morning, winter or summer, we'd see A. B., as we called him, striding by on his house calls, without an overcoat, or even galoshes when it snowed. His conviction was that "people wear too many clothes. The body can be trained to withstand heat and cold." Like George, he also believed that play is just as important as work. He persuaded us to join the square dancing club which met every week in his basement, and sometimes, instead of medicine, he tossed us the keys to his vacation cottage in the Blue Ridge mountains.

Most important of all, he taught his patients the secrets of cold showers. "If you do it right you'll love it," he promised. "Always start with hot water — never the cold, which would shock your system. Get warm and comfortable first, then gradually turn on the cold. As it strikes your body, slap your flesh, wiggle, sing, enjoy it. You'll come out feeling like a million dollars!"

He was so right. Ever since I started, the sheer exhilarating energy it evokes makes me want to leap out of bed every morning and head straight for the shower. I couldn't get through the day without it. And as I feel the brisk cold water on my skin, the blood coursing through my veins, it's like a fresh baptism of the spirit. I find myself offering up this little chant to heaven: "Thank you, Lord, for creating me, and giving me this wonderful body!... Thank you, George, for loving me....And thank you, Dr. A. B. Little!"

Third: *Stay as attractive as you can for as long as you can.* Don't let yourself go. The better you look the better you'll feel, even if there's nobody there to notice.

Every morning, right after my swim or shower, I fix my hair, put on my makeup, and dress in something comfortable but becoming, just as I did for George. How I wish I could have done this for my first husband — I believe it might have made a difference in our marriage. But with four children to get breakfast for and off to school, it simply wasn't possible (although I always did fix myself up later, by the time they got home).

Now I've gotten into the habit. And whether anybody ever looks at me or not, I want to feel good about myself, even on my morning walks to feed the birds and squirrels. They won't care, and neither will the occasional fishermen going by in their boats, or even stopping to cast and fish close by. But *I* care because all day, whenever I look in a mirror, I have to look at *me*.

These walks before breakfast are themselves invigorating and healing, a time when God has rouged the cheeks of morning and dressed the day in its brightest feathered garments of red-bellied woodpeckers, and blue jays and cardinals and redpolls, and goldfinches and yellow canaries — too many to name, all flying and flapping and singing and chirping to cheer you on....

In spring or summer I pick the wildflowers. In fall or early winter, when even the jaunty green grass is fading, like ladies whose hair is graying, I often pick the weeds. Some of them are tall and slender as wands and so beautiful in silhouette that I make an arrangement of them for the windows. Marveling that God should lavish his artistry on that humble growth, a weed which we consider only a nuisance to be whacked down and thrown away.

And sometimes there are surprises — even little miracles it seems. One very cold day in December as I walked the frozen ground, I could hardly believe my eyes. For there before me a *dandelion* was blooming, as bright yellow and sunny as spring! And just beyond it, a little cluster of four more, looking as perky and lively as a quartet about to sing. Still incredulous and delighted, I picked them to bring inside, leaving the first one standing alone, if only to prove they were *there.*

"Dandelions in December?" my daughter puzzled as I fixed the small bouquet. "Mother, didn't George always have fresh flowers on the table every morning? And even go to great lengths to find them for you, if necessary?"

"He sure did. If the store-bought ones ran out, I'd often see him in the yard, picking whatever he could find, no matter the weather, and sometimes raiding the neighbors."

We stared at each other a moment, laughing, but awed by the lovely possibility. Then Mickie voiced it for me: "This could be very symbolic, Mother. Maybe this is just his way of getting some special flowers for you today!"

Dandelions don't last long; but those I displayed in the kitchen window, heads held high, bent slightly toward the sun, lasted for over a week. Then they doffed their fluffy white hats to flirt with me and other admirers another five days before winds and grandchildren blew them away....

I realize how lucky I am to have so much space. But wherever you are, get up as early as you can, whenever you can, and go outdoors to walk as far as you can without tiring — whether in a park, a block down the street, or in your own yard, however small. Drink the sweet elixir of nature in the morning, the air so cool and sweet, the flowers and earth smelling so good you wish you could pack it up and share it with everyone who is lonely or sad about anything.

Breathe it deep, let it heal you. Even the scent of it is refreshing and restoring to body, mind, and emotions. A group of physicians and counselors are discovering the evidence to prove it. The person who is in tune with nature is usually in tune with life and better able to deal with loss — especially the loss of a deeply loved mate.

$\backsim$

Fourth: *Anticipate the day ahead.* Have something to get up early *for:* a project, job, hobby, cause, or avocation that really speaks to you and calls you into action.

Yes, you've earned the right to rest if you want to, to just read and enjoy the soaps or whatever you please. But it's common knowledge that the best antidote for loneliness or grief is keeping busy and helping somebody else.

The world is so full of suffering, the opportunities to serve are almost overwhelming: the homeless, the hungry, the lost, the abused or neglected children. Needs too long to list; too many to accomplish by yourself. As soon as possible, become a volunteer in the cause dearest to your heart. Or if you already belong, take more part in its activities. Nothing is more refreshing than the companionship of kind, caring friends who really want to help others.

My favorite charity has always been the Salvation Army. Its members are the dearest, warmest, happiest people I've ever known. Scanning my own life, I honestly believe that if the Lord hadn't wanted me to be a writer, I would have enlisted and hoped to be worthy of them. I did join their women's auxiliary even while raising my family of four children. And as each child got old enough, I let them take turns going with me to help with the special events. They particularly enjoyed the Doll Fair, and the Toy Center at Christmas, donning the bright red aprons we all were given and helping needy parents pick out gifts for their children.

It taught my own, not only how lucky they were, but something better: that it *is* more blessed to give than to receive, and even a lot more fun!

If you're not physically able to volunteer in this way, try to do something nice for at least one person every day. Call or write to somebody who needs to hear from you. Not about your misery and problems, but to be cheered and encouraged by what you have to say. Thank somebody fervently for what he or she has done for you. Pay a compliment to somebody who seldom gets a compliment from *anybody*. Use your talents and skills to bake or sew or create something pretty for an ailing or troubled friend.

Here too the opportunities are endless.

Fifth: *Think about what you have gained from this wonderful marriage, instead of what you have lost.*

Count them, add them up: the interesting people you wouldn't have met without your mate; the fascinating places you might never have seen on your travels; the vast shining fortune of experiences you had together. But even more important are the ways you changed each other.

No marriage ever leaves you the same as you were before — even a marriage that doesn't succeed. As one of my daughters told me about her divorce after only two turbulent years. "I don't regret it, Mother. We learned so much from each other. And who knows? Maybe something I said to Jack is helping him now. And I know that some of the things *he* said to me, even when angry, were actually good for me. We both had our faults, but God let us go through this. You can't *live* with someone, even a few years, without growing."

On a happier note, I am a better person because of my husband. Wiser, deeper, more aware — George taught me so much about life and love and God and the miracle of creation. Even of being born to occupy these incredible bodies, with minds to think and know the wonder of being on earth at all.

We taught *each other* so much, shaping and molding each other without even trying. And we, at least, we were so sublimely happy the memories are a joy to hug to my heart instead of sorrow.

Again I realize how richly blessed I am in having my writing to keep me busy — the work I was born to do, as essential to me as breathing. But the greatest blessing of all is the feeling that George is still with me wherever I am, on those morning walks, on a platform, or in the kitchen, that he knows and responds to whatever I think or have to say. So I don't really *miss* him so acutely any more — even the sound of his voice or his laughter — because I hear it all the time in my heart and in my head.

Like a lot of people, I talk to myself, and we seem to have these merry conversations:

"Oh, dear, just *look* what I've done, ruined a whole page, and I can't find the ones I just put down."

"Let it go. It's lunchtime, honey, time to quit."

"But I want to finish two more paragraphs."

"Don't worry, they'll wait, and I know you're hungry. Come on, doctor's orders."

I know that seems silly, but it's true for me and I don't care who knows it. Sometimes I remind myself of a woman whose huge Victorian house we used to pass on our way to school. She'd been married a long time, people said, and gone a little wacky after she lost her husband. She talked to him all the time, and even set a place for him at the table. I don't go that far, but I know how she felt.

Now I want to urge you: don't resign yourself to never seeing or feeling the presence of the one you love again. Talk to your beloved whenever you want to, if this comes naturally, and listen for your beloved's answers.

If you were truly soulmates, with a marriage made in heaven, you have every reason to be happy. So stay very close to God and wait patiently for your call to join your beloved when the time is ready.

Because a truly great love can never die. You will be together forever in Paradise!

Afterword

WILL YOU EVER HEAR FROM YOUR LOST LOVE AGAIN?

Prayer for Discernment

Dear God,

Please give us discernment.

Help us to know the difference

between true communication

with those we have lost,

and false prophets and seers

who would lead us astray.

Let us remember that if we do receive

such thrilling and joyful messages,

they are always a gift

that you have sent to comfort us,

and they come only because of you.

*W*ILL YOU EVER HEAR from your lost love again? That is the question so often asked. According to recent surveys, almost half the bereaved people in America believe they *have* had such communication. It was the subject of a television special on the program *20/20* in mid-April 1996, which consisted solely of individuals describing how it had happened to them.

There is also an abundance of books about such phenomena. One of them, *Whispers of Love,* by Mitch Finley, cites the famous example of C. S. Lewis and his encounter with his wife, Joy, after her death (as described in Lewis's own book *A Grief Observed*). He also speaks of the writings of Catherine Marshall, widow of the famous Scottish minister Peter Marshall, who died while serving as official chaplain to Congress.

It was my privilege to know Catherine Marshall. She welcomed me warmly when I first moved to Washington, D.C., and became a very dear friend. She was one of a little group of women writers, all professionals, who met about once a month for lunch, to discuss our work and sometimes our woes. By that time she had already written her best-selling books about Peter, and I had written several novels as well as my first book of prayers, *I've Got to Talk to Somebody, God.*

At the moment she was working on a book dramatizing the true story of her mother as a young girl struggling to teach school in the primitive backwoods of the Ozark mountains. It was different from her other books, and such a challenge; she was both nervous and excited as she read parts of it to us.

She asked me to drive with her one day to meet her mother at Evergreen, as they called the beautiful farm and ancient mansion near Leesburg, Virginia, which Catherine had bought and personally restored for her parents when her father, Reverend Wood, retired. Both of them were warm and wonderful. But my attention was focused on the delightful woman who was the real-life "Christy." I thought I might do a story about her for the column I was writing for the *Washington Evening Star.*

Neither of us dreamed that *Christy* would also become a film and the inspiration for one of the most popular TV series ever produced. But of all the books Catherine ever wrote, the most important for me after losing George has been *To Live Again.* In it she describes her search for hope and meaning after Peter died and devotes an entire chapter to the question "Is There Life after Death?" She found a number of notes and letters Peter had written to people who had asked him this question, in which he states his own conviction that those who have left us can and do come back "and are with us still in different form, and communicate with us in different ways. . . . It takes time and the grace of God and a simple Christian faith to feel the presence of our beloved departed, but that in itself is a comfort and consolation that will fill up the vacuum in your life. . . . I believe in the communion of saints."

In this remarkable book Catherine describes in detail the research she did on the Apostles' Creed to determine the meaning of the familiar term "communion of saints." She discovered that from the beginning of the Ancient Church, the word "saints" always referred to *everyone* who has died, and not merely to those officially "canonized" or pronounced worthy of the title. This creed states that we should not only pray for the souls of the departed, but ask them for help when we need it. For her this proved to be the most significant and reassuring of all.

Close as she and Peter had been, she had not personally experienced the wonderful contact with his spirit that so many people had predicted she would, in telling their own exciting stories. But her faith in his presence was strong, and whenever she had a difficult problem, she asked God to let him join her in prayer for its resolution. And in every case, the crisis passed. "One door closed, another opened, the good appeared. It was significant beyond imagining."

During that early period of our friendship, Catherine's loving eyes seemed to follow me, and we had some serious talks. One day I told her that in seeking a deeper faith, I had been led to the charismatic movement. At the urging of my teenage daughter, I began to attend a "born again" church which denounces anything having to do with the occult and preaches the baptism of the Holy Spirit with its priceless gift of speaking in tongues. There we both received that thrilling gift just before she went away to college.

And I'm convinced it saved her life!

For one night in Boston, while she was walking back to the dormitory alone, a man came out of the shadows, grabbed her, and tried to drag her into an alley. She screamed, of course, but nobody heard, and in the violent struggle that followed, she called out desperately for God's help, in tongues.

Instantly her assailant released her and backed away. However, as she ran screaming down the street, he pursued her, and again terrified she cried out in tongues, begging the Holy Spirit to save her.

This time, muttering "Who *are* you?" the man let her go completely, turned, and fled.

Catherine was nodding and smiling faintly as she listened to my story, and her eyes were bright as she reached out to grip my hand. "Yes, of course," she said simply. "Evil can't live in the Presence." Thus I learned that she herself was a born-again Christian.

Although she kept a low profile about this, it is very clear in the last book she wrote, *The Helper.* In it she describes and explains the Holy Spirit, which so many churches ignore and so few people understand, and how it can protect us from the demons that are unleashed when we follow false prophets and deal with forbidden spirits that would alter God's plan. That is all we need to remember.

But communion with those we have loved and lost is not forbidden in the Bible. From the earliest days of Pentecost we are encouraged to pray for and with them. And if other communion comes naturally, open your mind and heart to receive it with thanksgiving. It is a gift from God.

OF RELATED INTEREST

———■———

Paula D'Arcy
GIFT OF THE RED BIRD
A Spiritual Encounter
"This is one of the loveliest books I have ever read,
touching on our human need to know God in the strangest,
darkest places." —Madeleine L'Engle

0-8245-1590-0; $14.95 hc

Jean Vanier
JESUS, THE GIFT OF LOVE
A luminous retelling of the life of Jesus of Nazareth by one
of this century's most revered spiritual writers.

0-8245-1593-5; $12.95 pb

———■———

*At your bookstore or, to order directly from the publisher,
please send check or money order (including $1.00 for the first book
plus $1.00 for each additional book) to:*

THE CROSSROAD PUBLISHING COMPANY
370 LEXINGTON AVENUE, NEW YORK, NY 10017

We hope you enjoyed Still by Your Side. *Thank you for reading it.*

crossroad